Celebrate!

Gifts of Time with Grandma

Over 200 Delightful Activities to Enjoy with Your Grandchild

Celebrate!

Gifts of Time with Grandma

Over 200 Delightful Activities to Enjoy with Your Grandchild

Elaine Bezanson

and

Kathryn Wallace

Illustrated by Bev Weismann

iUniverse, Inc.

New York   Bloomington

iUniverse books may be ordered through booksellers or by contacting:

iUniverse
1663 Liberty Drive
Bloomington, IN 47403
www.iuniverse.com
1-800-Authors (1-800-288-4677)

Because of the dynamic nature of the Internet, any Web addresses or links contained in this book may have changed since publication and may no longer be valid. The views expressed in this work are solely those of the author and do not necessarily reflect the views of the publisher, and the publisher hereby disclaims any responsibility for them.

ISBN: 978-1-4401-4528-5 (sc)
ISBN: 978-1-4401-4529-2 (ebook)

Printed in the United States of America

iUniverse rev. date: 07/14/2009

To our six wonderful grandchildren Nathan, Anna, Noah, Tennyson, Maya, and Zoë

Introduction

Celebrate! Gifts of Time with Grandma is designed by two enthusiastic grandmas to enhance the delights of grandparenting. A grandma has time, energy, and infinite patience, but sometimes she runs out of ideas. Our hope is that you will flip through the pages of *Celebrate!* and find a myriad of creative, easy activities for your grandchild's visit. These activities can be accomplished by grandpas as well as grandmas, and also by aunts, uncles, cousins, friends, and babysitters.

Our suggested activities are divided by category: Music, Cooking, Nature, Amusements, Arts and Crafts, Reading and Storytelling, Imagining, Water Play, Science and Logic, More Fun, Long-Distance Grandchild, and Pre Baby New Baby. Within each category, the activities are organized by age, beginning with activities for the youngest grandchild. The age ranges are *only* suggestions; you and your grandchild will know if and when the activity is appropriate.

For us, there are no sex-role stereotypes. The activities we present are based on the child's interests, not on expectations of gender. We have alternated the use of the pronouns "he" and "she" throughout the book to reinforce our intention of non-gendered activities. The ideas presented in *Celebrate!* are not intended to "teach," but if learning happens as a result, fantastic! We do not intend to "preach," but if your relationship with your grandchild is enhanced, fantastic!

Go for it. Grab a project, try it with your grandchild, and see where it leads. These activities, like cooking recipes, can be spiced to suit your tastes or they may evolve into a totally new recipe. We hope you will use the final page of each section, "Grandma Notes and Ideas," to record which activities worked well, how you changed the activity, and any new ideas to try on another day.

Best wishes from two fun-loving grandmas who *Celebrate!* with their grandchildren.

Table of Contents

Acknowledgements

Grandma Elaine and Grandma Kathryn would like to acknowledge several individuals who were especially helpful and supportive during the writing and editing of *Celebrate!*

To our six grandchildren, Nathan, Anna, Noah, Tennyson, Maya, and Zoë, bouquets of love and hugs for their very existence, their inspiration, and their willingness to test these activities.

To our friend and artist Bev Weismann for her willingness to join us in this endeavor and for her skills at making the book more friendly and more fun.

To our friends Katherine and John Moyers for their photography skills, their photo editing advice, and their general enthusiasm.

To Ellie Densen, Anne Hesse, Jean Hines, and Linda Rotman for their initial read of the manuscript and for their continued support.

To Sandy Schantz and Ginny Clemons for fantastic ideas for projects and for their on-going support.

To our daughters Melissa Bezanson Shultz and Rachel Wallace Tellez and to Linda Ely for reading and editing the final manuscript and for their encouragement and enthusiasm.

To our husbands Pete Wallace and Randy Bezanson for their unfailing confidence in our abilities.

Making Music When You Are Not Musical
Newborn-10 years

Supplies: Compact discs of children's music
              Compact disc player

There are many wonderful compact discs available specifically for babies or toddlers. Look for vocalists such as Raffi, Laurie Berkner, Sara Hickman, the Cedarmont Kids, and Pete Seeger. Consider also a Sesame Street album or *Free to Be You and Me* by Marlo Thomas.

Listen to the discs ahead of time, selecting the songs that might appeal to your grandchild. Learn the words. Encourage your grandchild to sing along to the music. A new star may be born.

The Singing Grandma
Newborn–2 years

Supplies: Grandma's voice
                        Tape recorder or computer with microphone
                        Blank tape or compact disc

Relearn songs from your childhood and songs you sang to your children. Record these songs in your own voice. Make two copies of the disc or tape, one to send home with your grandchild and one to keep at your house.

Silly Grandma
3 months–2 years

Supplies: Grandpa's lap

Grandpa holds the child on his lap facing outward. Grandma stands in front of the baby to act out songs or nursery rhymes like "I'm a Little Teapot," "The Itsy Bitsy Spider," or any others you remember. Both Grandma and Grandpa sing the words and laugh a lot.

Music as a Bedtime Ritual
3 months–10 years

Supplies: A few extra minutes at bedtime
                        Songs from memory

There is nothing as relaxing as a few bedtime songs. Sing *to* the young grandchild and *with* the older grandchild. Some of the songs may become special traditions shared by you and your grandchild.

Drumboree
12 months+

Supplies: Empty containers with lids
      Wooden spoons

Help your grandchild make a collection of drums from empty coffee cans, shoeboxes, oatmeal boxes, or cocoa containers. You can decorate the sides of the drums by gluing on felt or construction paper. Use a wooden spoon to beat out a rhythm. Encourage your grandchild to copy the rhythm or make up one of his own. Experiment with different sized containers to listen for differing sounds. Place objects inside the containers to see which objects change the sound.

I've Got Rhythm I
12 months+

Supplies: Items your grandchild can clash together
      Rhythmic music on compact disc

Gather household items such as wooden spoons, pans, and metal measuring cups. Play music that encourages banging and rhythm like the marches of John Phillip Sousa. March around the room with the "instruments," making rhythm and joy.

Making Music Traditions
12 months+

Supplies: Pen and paper
                         Grandma's memory

Sometimes when it comes time for singing your favorite songs with your grandchildren, memory fails. Keep a list of songs to try with your grandchildren. Or have your grandchildren help you make the list. Some songs will be instant hits. You can note your grandchild's preferences and reactions. It's surprising what the children end up loving. "Daisy, Daisy, Give Me Your Answer, Do" and "Zippity Doo Dah" are perennial favorites. Leave no stone unturned. Your grandchild may even enjoy your favorite Beatles songs.

Toddler Tones: End the Phrase
15 months+

Supplies: One singing Grandma
                         Toddler in a vocal mood

Your grandchild has probably heard many songs while being cuddled, rocked to sleep, and entertained as a baby. Now it's time for her to participate. Pick simple tunes that you know the child has heard. Examples are "Twinkle, Twinkle Little Star"; "My Bonnie Lies Over the Ocean"; "A Hunting We Will Go"; "The Itsy Bitsy Spider." Sing the entire song to the child several times. Then pause just before the end of a phrase. "Twinkle, twinkle, little _____." Encourage the child to say "star." Continue with "How I wonder what you _____." Soon the child will understand the way this game is played, and she will finish the musical phrases for you.

Waltz of the Flowers
3 years+

Supplies: Recording of "Waltz of the Flowers"
A large space in which to move

Play a recording of Tchaikovsky's "Waltz of the Flowers" from *The Nutcracker Suite*. Help your grandchild imagine he is a small flower in the ground, awakened by the beautiful music. The flower grows, and he leaps and dances around the room.

Combining physical activity and drama with music can be accomplished with many musical pieces. Other examples are *The Grand Canyon Suite* by Ferde Grofé and *Peter and the Wolf* by Sergei Prokofiev.

I've Got Rhythm II
3 years+

Supplies: Toy instruments
Rhythmic music on compact disc
Tape recorder or computer with microphone

Purchase some toy instruments such as a drum, kazoo, whistle, triangle, rhythm blocks, sand blocks, or rhythm sticks. Encourage your grandchild to pound out the rhythm to marches or polkas. Record her rhythmic accompaniment. Grandma can serve as "master of ceremonies" on the recording, announcing the piece and the performer. You can also record an older child playing her own musical instrument.

Listening to the performance is a real thrill for the child. Give Mom or Dad the tape or compact disc as a gift.

Name That Tune
3-10 years

Supplies: A Grandma who hums

Hum a familiar tune and see if your grandchild can name it. Be prepared to "perform" many songs for him to guess.

This game can be played using an instrumental compact disc, by plunking out the song on a piano, or by strumming the song on a guitar. Humming, however, is the most flexible way to do this. You can hum in a car, in a boat, at bedtime, and even during bath time.

Row Your Boat
3 years+

Supplies: Grandma's voice and memory for rounds

Singing in rounds is challenging. Children love to give it a try. Begin with "Row, Row, Row Your Boat" and progress to "Are You Sleeping" and "Three Blind Mice." Then continue on to more difficult songs like "White Coral Bells" and "Kookaburra." Round-singing is most easily learned if Grandma and Grandpa demonstrate first, and then Grandpa sings along with the child to help her stay on track.

Water Glass Chimes
4 years+

Supplies: Seven identical, tall glasses
Pitcher of water
Long-handled, metal spoon
An ear with good musical pitch

Set up a musical scale by pouring differing quantities of water into each of seven glasses. The highest note on the scale will be the glass containing the least amount of water. Grandma can set up the scale prior to a young grandchild's visit. Older children may wish to experiment with the tones themselves.

Using the spoon, play simple songs like "Twinkle, Twinkle." The child musician may become quite fascinated and reproduce several tunes. He might even compose his own.

Grandma's Notes and Ideas

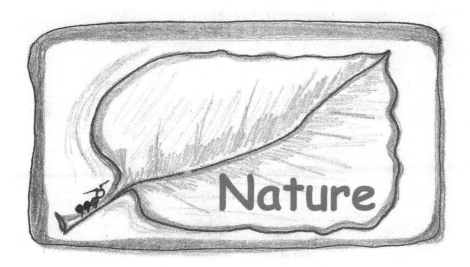

Playing in the Leaves
12 months–10 years

Supplies: A fall day with leaves on the ground
                  Child-sized, plastic rake
                  Adult rake

Rake up a pile of leaves and jump in them with your grandchild. Kick and throw the leaves. Have him bury you in leaves. Collect a few leaves to glue onto paper as a memento of the day.

Day Trek
18 months–5 years

Supplies: Plastic container with air holes poked in the lid
Bag to carry treasures

Go on a neighborhood hike in search of treasures. Talk about the flowers, the trees, and the bugs that you see as well as the birds that you hear. Try catching a bug or two in the container. Allow your grandchild to carry home some special mementos of the hike such as pinecones, rocks, grass, or leaves. A great end to the hike is "rest time" in the backyard where you and your grandchild lie on your backs in the grass and find shapes in the clouds.

Hello, Birdie
18 months+

Supplies: Bagel
Piece of string, yarn or ribbon
Peanut butter
Solid vegetable shortening
Birdseed
Bird identification book, optional
Compact disc of bird songs, optional

Tie a piece of string through the bagel for a hanger. Mix 3 T peanut butter (creamy or chunky) with 1 T vegetable shortening. Spread the mixture on all sides of the bagel. Roll the bagel in bird seed. Hang it outside and hope for birds. Talk about different kinds of birds and their songs. If you get squirrels instead, enjoy watching their antics.

Sand Secrets
18 months–10 years

Supplies: A sandy beach
              Buckets and shovels

If you are fortunate to be with your grandchild on a beach, you will hear her giggle when you bury her bare feet in the sand. Ask, "Where are your toes?"

Other sand activities:

- Show her how to bury *your* bare feet. Wiggle, wiggle your toes to escape.
- Dig a large hole in the sand, fill with water, and set the baby in her own pool.
- Encourage your grandchild to carry buckets of sand to bury Grandma's legs.
- Cover an older child's legs, arms, and trunk with sand.
- Volunteer to be a sand mummy yourself, if you are brave enough.
- Build a sand castle village using buckets as molds, rocks as ramparts, and water for a moat.

Nature's Jewels
18 months–5 years

Supplies: Masking tape
                      Scissors
                      Wagon, optional

Wrap a piece of masking tape around your grandchild's wrist, sticky side up. Take a nature hike or wagon ride around the neighborhood to search for interesting, lightweight items to attach to his bracelet. You can gather small leaves, dandelions, or tree bark. When you return home, discuss each item, where he found it, and why he chose it for his bracelet.

Night Hike
2 years+

Supplies: Ingredients for homemade cocoa
                      Library books about night sights and sounds
                      Flashlight

Let your grandchild stay up past her bedtime. Go for a walk in the dark of night. Look at the stars and the moon. Listen to the night sounds. Shine a flashlight on trees or other familiar objects. In early summer, you can catch fireflies in a glass jar and watch them light up. Follow your adventure with homemade cocoa and a story about the moon or about night animals. Book suggestions are *Papa Please Bring Me the Moon* by Eric Carle or *A Night in the Country* by Cynthia Rylant.

Falling Leaves
2-5 years

Supplies: Glue
                Construction paper
                Colorful leaves
                White paper
                Tape
                Crayons

Take a fall hike with your grandchild to gather beautiful leaves of various shapes and colors.

After your hike, you can:

- Make a collage by gluing leaves on a piece of construction paper.
- Make a person or critter by gluing a large leaf on construction paper for the body. Use smaller leaves for the head, legs, and arms.
- Create a leaf image by taping the stem of a leaf to a table. Cover the leaf with a sheet of plain white paper. Rub a crayon on the paper. The leaf shape will magically appear.
- Read *The Busy Little Squirrel* by Nancy Tafuri (2–4 years); *Leaf Man* by Lois Ehlert (2–5 years); or *Frederick* by Leo Lionni (3–5 years).

Go Green
2–10 years

Supplies: Small tree to plant
Shovel
Potting soil
Large rock
Permanent marker

Take your grandchild to a greenhouse to select a small, hardy tree to plant in a special place in your yard. If you live on a wooded lot, dig a sapling to transplant. After you and your grandchild have planted the tree, mark its location with the rock. Write her name on the rock with permanent marker. Each time your grandchild comes to visit she can observe her own tree in your yard. Watching it grow and thrive will provide enjoyment to you and your grandchild for years to come.

Camping IN
3 years+

Supplies: A screened porch
Air mattresses
Sleeping bags
Flashlights, snacks, and stories to tell

Blow up the air mattresses and lay out the sleeping bags on the screened porch. Make a lot of effort toward an "outdoor" experience with flashlights, snacks, and stories. Listen to the bugs, the birds, and the owls. Have every intention of camping there all night. Perhaps you will.

Flower Power
3-8 years

Supplies: White flowers
                     Vase
                     Food coloring
                     Patience

Purchase or gather white flowers. Carnations, mums, daisies, or Queen Anne's lace are good choices. Add 20 drops of food coloring and ½ cup warm water to a flower vase. Cut at least two inches from the stems of the flowers. Place the flowers in the vase. You and your grandchild can watch the gradual power of the flowers as the white petals take on the color of the water.

Flowers continually take in water through their stems. The water evaporates through the petals leaving behind the food coloring. Patience is necessary since you won't see results for about 24 hours.

Nuts to You
4 years+

Supplies: Nuts in their shells
                     Nut cracker and a pick
                     Bowls for the meats and the shells

Most grocery stores stock unshelled nuts beginning in the fall. Your grandchild will enjoy selecting a few of each kind. At home, show your grandchild how to use the nutcracker to reveal the edible nut inside the shell. Discuss the different varieties, their shapes, and textures. Help your grandchild crack open all the shells and extract the small pieces with the pick. Encourage him to taste each variety and to select a favorite.

Monarch Miracle
4 years+

Supplies: Space in your garden
                     Milkweed plant
                     Clear plastic berry container with lid
                     Patience

In the spring, purchase a milkweed plant to place in your garden. The milkweed plant attracts the monarch caterpillar, which will eat the leaves. When you see a caterpillar, place it, along with several leaves, in the plastic container. Keep the container in the shade outside or on a screened porch. (Air conditioning is not healthy for the caterpillar.)

The caterpillar will eventually turn into a chrysalis and later emerge as a gorgeous monarch butterfly. Release the butterfly outside.

The entire evolution takes approximately 12 days, depending on the outdoor temperatures. There are some exquisite pictures of this process on the Internet, if you are not able to witness it for yourself.

A Thing of Beauty is a Joy to Behold
4 years+

Supplies: Flowers for drying
                     Flower press or many heavy books
                     Paper towels

Gather flowers with thin petals such as daisies, columbine, or Queen Anne's lace. Place the flowers between paper towels to absorb the moisture. Then help your grandchild place the sheets of flowers in a press or under a stack of heavy books. A week later you and your grandchild can remove the flowers from the "press." The dried flowers can be glued to paper and framed as a gift. Queen Anne's lace makes a particularly lovely framed piece.

Welcome, Peter Rabbit
4 years+

Supplies: Plants and/or seeds which are certain to grow
An area for your grandchild's garden

It is a lucky grandchild who has his own corner of Grandma's garden to tend. If a tilled area is not possible, provide several large pots filled with soil.

Let the child be creative in planning his garden, choosing his own combination of vegetables and flowers. Take photos of the results. Find an opportunity to talk about what changes to his garden he might make the following year.

Optional equipment may include child-sized garden clogs, trowels, hats, and gloves.

My Secret (Miniature) Garden
4-10 years

Supplies: Sturdy cardboard box about 3-inches deep
Black garbage bag
Potting soil
Miniature plants
Miscellaneous items to
represent garden features

To create a miniature garden, line the box with the garbage bag. Fill the box with potting soil.

Take your grandchild to a garden center to buy a few miniature plants to serve as trees, shrubs, and flowering bushes. Use a mirror or jar lid as a pond or pool. Use pieces of gravel for landscape rock. Buttons make great stepping stones. Doll house items such as a bird house, a swing set, or a picnic table can decorate the garden.

Chained with Flowers
5-10 years

Supplies: Clover flowers or dandelions
                   Safety pin, optional

Introduce your grandchild to the simple pleasure of making necklaces from nature. Gather bunches of clover flowers or dandelions.

The stems of clover flowers are flexible and can be tied together with a knot. Knot the stem end of one flower just beneath the bloom of another. Repeat until the necklace is the desired length. Make a circle by knotting the first stem to the last bloom.

For dandelions or other flowers with thick stems, use your fingernail to poke a slit through the center of the stem. Then, insert another stem into the slit and pull it all the way through. Repeat, making a slit in the newly inserted stem and continue with this method until the necklace is the desired length. To finish a circle, make a slit in the last stem and insert the stem of the first flower into it or safety pin the ends together.

Grandma's Notes and Ideas

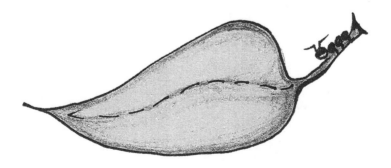

Splish! Splash! I
6 months+

Supplies: Plastic containers
                        Measuring cups and spoons
                        Hose or faucet

Set your grandchild in the grass or on a deck or patio. Surround her with water-filled containers. Show her how to pour from one container to another. Watch her delight as she pours and dumps water everywhere.

Rub a Dub Dub
9 months-5 years

Supplies: Sink or bucket full of warm water
                    Liquid dish soap
                    Stool or chair for the child to stand on

A sink or bucket full of water provides many opportunities for fun. Your grandchild can:

- Make suds with the dish soap. Lift and blow the suds.
- Use plastic containers to pour water and suds from one to another.
- Wash plastic dishes.
- Wash doll clothes and lay them out to dry.
- Wash stuffed animals.

After the water play, read *I Love You, Bunny Rabbit* by Shulamith Levey Oppenheim.

Splish! Splash! II
15 months+

Supplies: Hose
                    Sprinkler
                    Bathing suits
                    A hot day

Turn on the sprinkler and run through it with your grandchild. You may wish to share stories of your childhood sprinkler fun.

Faux Painting
18 months+

Supplies: 2- or 3-inch-wide paint brush
                      Bucket of water
                      A warm summer day

Give your grandchild a bucket full of water and a paint brush. He can "paint" the porch steps, the garage floor, or any exterior surface. When the child is finished and the surface is dry, he may wish to "paint" it all over again.

Car Wash
3-10 years

Supplies: A hot summer day
                      One dirty car
                      Bucket of soapy water
                      Garden hose
                      Lots of rags and sponges
                      Car wax, optional

For fun write "Wash Me!" in the dust on your car. Ask your grandchild to help you gather the necessary items for an outdoor car wash. Wash the car with rags and soapy water, rinse with the hose, and dry. An older child can learn how to use car wax to polish Grandma's car to mirrored shine. Be prepared to get wet. As an alternative, drive to a "wash-it-yourself" car wash and have your grandchild help you clean the car.

Grandma's Notes and Ideas

Me Too
9 months–2 years

Supplies: Cheerios or other finger food

Provide your grandchild with a bowl of finger food. Then ask, "May I have some?" If your grandchild doesn't respond, simply guide her hand to your mouth. Always say "Thank you" as you chew in an exaggerated fashion. Take turns feeding each other. Pretend to feed stuffed animals or dolls.

My Fork, My Spoon
12 months+

Supplies Toddler fork and spoon

Purchase a set of toddler utensils. Prepare forkable and spoonable snacks such as Jell-O blocks, thick pudding, and soft bread cubes so your grandchild can practice using his utensil skills.

Measure and Pour
12 months–2½ years

Supplies: Cornmeal or sand
                      Plastic tablecloth
                      Unbreakable measuring cups
                      Various sizes of unbreakable containers
                      Spoons
                      Funnel

Place your grandchild in the center of the tablecloth with the utensils and a container of cornmeal or sand. (Use cornmeal for children who are still mouthing everything they touch.) Show her how to measure out some cornmeal and to pour it into another container.

Cookies?
2–6 years

Supplies: Big bowl
                      Any cookie recipe
                      Cookie sheet
                      Measuring cups and spoons
                      Stirring spoon

Cooking with children is great fun, but sometimes Grandma just can't handle the mess. Pretend cookies might be just right for you. Read each recipe ingredient to your grandchild and have him measure and bring the pretend item to the bowl, stirring after each addition. Form into pretend cookies. "Bake" and "serve" them on a tray to Grandpa or other guests. Older children often enjoy this activity if they think they are entertaining younger siblings or cousins.

Cookie Treats I
2-10 years

Supplies: Cookie ingredients*
                 Necessary utensils

Depending on the child's age, baking cookies can be easy or more difficult.

- For the youngest grandchildren (2–3 years), you can enlist their help in baking refrigerated dough from the store.
- For slightly older grandchildren (3–4 years), you can mix dough ahead and let the child dig out spoonfuls to set on a cookie sheet.
- Children from 4 on up can assist in the preparation of the dough.
- Eventually your grandchild will enjoy using the mixer himself and be ready to make cookies all on his own.

*If you want to snack on the cookie dough, be aware that raw eggs are unsafe to eat. Pasteurized eggs are available.

Cookie Treats II
2½-10 years

Supplies: Sugar cookie dough
Cake decorating sprinkles
Colored sugar
Small candies or chocolate chips
Frosting in a can

Purchase ready-to-bake sugar cookie dough and a can of white frosting. (The cream cheese variety tastes great.) For the younger child, you can bake the cookies ahead of time according to the package directions and let them cool. Older grandchildren may wish to participate in the baking.

Give your grandchild a spreading spatula and small bowls of frosting, sprinkles, colored sugar, and candies. Let her decorate each cookie in any way she wishes.

You can color the frosting with food coloring. You can roll out the dough and use cookie cutters for the shapes. You can make your favorite sugar cookie dough from scratch.

A Lick on a Stick
2½-10 years

Supplies: Paper cups or Popsicle molds
                        Popsicle sticks
                        Blender
                        Ingredients for the recipe you choose

Frozen treats are easy and tasty. The only downside is that you and your grandchild must wait a while before enjoying them.

Recipe I: 1 cup fresh or frozen strawberries, cleaned, topped and blended. Blend in 1 cup orange juice and sugar or honey to taste.

Recipe II: 2 cups fresh blueberries, raspberries, strawberries, and sliced bananas, puréed. Blend in 2 cups plain or vanilla yogurt and ¼ cup white sugar.

Fill small paper cups ¾ full. Cover each cup with foil. Insert the stick through the foil and into the center of the filling. Freeze for 4 hours or overnight. (If you purchase molds, use as directed.)

Try creating your own concoctions with different ingredients.

Tea Party Fit For a Queen
3 years+

Supplies: Child-sized tea set
Weak tea, water, or juice
Pretend or real cookies or other snack food

A tea party is an endless source of imagination and joy. It can be completely pretend or completely real. The tea party can be elaborate with invitations and place cards or simply an informal gathering. Guests can be real people, stuffed animals, dolls, or imaginary friends. Entertainment can be conversation, music, or stories.

Yummy Memories
3 years+

Supplies: Ingredients for your treat

Did your mother or father cook special treats for you? Did you cook special treats for your children? Share the recipes and the cooking with your grandchild. Family traditions might include Rice Krispies Treats, fudge, taffy, ice cream, Jell-O salad, tapioca pudding, or S'mores.

Edible Creatures
3-8 years

Supplies: Frozen bread dough

Thaw frozen bread dough overnight or in the microwave. Your grandchild can sculpt the dough into shapes of his choice: a sun, a moon, a bunny rabbit, an octopus, or a fantasy critter. Because the dough begins to rise almost immediately, use your hands rather than a cookie cutter for shaping.

Paint the creature with food coloring, if your grandchild desires. Bake, checking frequently for doneness with a toothpick. Baking time depends on the thickness of the sculpture. The child is proud to serve the "creature" for breakfast, snack time, or dinner.

We All Scream for Ice Cream
3 years+

Supplies: One cake mix
Ice cream cones, *flat* on the bottom
Muffin pan
Icing, sprinkles, mini-chips

Prepare the cake mix as directed. Place the ice cream cones in a muffin pan using crumpled foil to stabilize the cone. Fill cones halfway up with batter (about ¼ cup).

Bake at 350°, for about 25 minutes. Test for doneness with a toothpick. Cool, then frost and decorate. Teach your grandchild the saying "You scream. I scream. We all scream for ice cream."

Faux Mixing and Baking
3 years+

Supplies: One flexible grandma
                Lots of plastic containers
                A warm summer day
                A generous supply of dirt and water

Making mud pies, mud cakes, and mud cookies can last an entire afternoon. Mix dirt and water to the right consistency. Shape the mud into muffins, cookies, or pies. Leave time for a good soak in the tub.

Making Salsa, Olé
3 years+

Supplies: Tomatoes, green peppers, onions, green chilies
                Options: Black olives, black beans, grated cheese
                Sharp knife
                Several small bowls
                Tortilla chips

Making salsa is a matter of preference. Chop the selected food items into small pieces. (The age of your grandchild dictates who does the chopping.) Place each type of food in its own bowl. Let your grandchild spoon ingredients from the bowls into a mixing bowl, making salsa in the proportions she chooses.

Bring out the chips. Dip, taste, and discuss what she might like to change. Try a new set of proportions with the same ingredients or additional ingredients until she loves her tasty creation. Write down the recipe.

Lemonade Entrepreneurs
4 years+

Supplies: Table and chairs
Lemonade and ice
Disposable cups
Coins for making change
Cookies, optional

Help your grandchild set up a lemonade stand. A busy sidewalk is the ideal spot. If you live in a more isolated location, call on your friends and relatives to stop by. It is important for him to have a little success in his first business venture.

When he is older, you may wish to discuss the cost of the purchased items and to help him determine the amount necessary to charge the customers.

To Market, To Market
5 years+

Supplies: Recipes
Paper to make a shopping list
Calculator

When planning to cook with your grandchild, take him to the grocery store to select the items to be used in the project. Have him read the recipe, make the grocery list, and then shop for the items with you.

An older grandchild can use the calculator to figure out the price per unit of weight or to add up the total cost. This is an opportunity to share any knowledge you have about store brands versus name brands and quality versus price.

Guess Who's Coming to Dinner?
6 years+

Supplies: Grandma's recipes

Pre-select some easy-to-make recipes from your collection in the categories of main dish, salad, and dessert. Allow the child to choose what she is going to make from the presented choices. Depending on her age, she can cook the recipes with no help from Grandma, some help from Grandma, or *a lot* of help from Grandma. Invite her parents or friends to the dinner and let the child receive the praise she deserves.

Grandma's Notes and Ideas

Silly Sounds, Funny Faces
6 weeks–12 months

Supplies: Grandma

Let your grandchild bring out the actress in you. Make all the animal sounds you can think of. Accompany the sounds with actions, if you are so inclined. Make faces of all kinds like sad, happy, sleepy, and mad. If you are lucky, you will generate a smile or a giggle.

What's Inside?
18 months–3 years

Supplies: Empty boxes

Without your grandchild's knowledge, place familiar objects inside several boxes. You can choose a favorite toy for one box, some cereal for another, and a book for another. Ask your grandchild to shake the box. Talk about the sound it makes. Ask your grandchild to guess what's inside. Then let him open the box to see if he's guessed correctly.

As an alternative, put a familiar object in a paper sack. Ask your grandchild to guess what's inside by feeling it without peeking.

Let It Snow
18 months+

Supplies: Plain white paper to wad up
                    White Styrofoam packing peanuts

Make "snowballs" with wadded up paper to toss at each other. Or create a snowstorm using the packing peanuts. These two activities may be combined for a real blizzard!

Talk about winter activities and read some winter books. Book suggestions are *The Snowy Day* by Ezra Jack Keats, *The Snowman* by Raymond Briggs, or *Snow!* by P.D. Eastman.

It's a Zoo
18 months+

Supplies: Every stuffed animal available

                  Plastic laundry baskets or empty boxes

Gather all your grandchild's stuffed animals into a zoo. Make cages under chairs, from laundry baskets, or from boxes. The animals can make noises, perform tricks, or form a parade. Older children may want Grandma to label each animal's habitat. Great books to accompany your zoo play are *Good Night Gorilla* by Peggy Rathmann (1½–3 years); *Gorilla! Gorilla!* by Jeanne Willis (3–6 years); or *Never, Ever Shout in a Zoo* by Karma Wilson (3–6 years).

Mini Charades I
2½-5 years

Supplies: Grandma

                  Grandchild

The guessing game charades can be played by young children. Grandma pretends to be an animal familiar to the child such as a monkey, a cat, or a bumblebee. Then Grandma asks, "Can you guess what Grandma is?" After he guesses correctly, Grandma pretends to be another animal.

Then introduce an animal for your grandchild to act out. "Can you be a bumblebee?" "Can you be a cat?"

Next the child thinks of his own animals to imitate. Grandma guesses, and hopefully she will have some correct answers.

Retro Unbirthday Party
3 years+

Supplies: Equipment to play the games you select

Invite Grandpa and any other close-at-hand friends, either your age or your grandchild's age, to an unbirthday party. Play old-fashioned games. Some suggestions are Button Button Who's Got the Button, Clothespin Drop, Hot Potato, Red Light-Green Light, Simon Says, Musical Chairs, or Pin the Tail on the Donkey. An elaborate unbirthday party could include invitations, cupcakes, and party decorations, all planned and carried out with your grandchild.

Cinderella and Beyond
3 years+

Supplies: Women's old clothes, purses, jewelry
                Men's ties, hats, shirts, shoes, briefcases, wallet
                Any type of uniform

By saving that appliquéd T-shirt, the boots you loved ten years ago, or the hats you inherited from your parents, you will have an array of dress-up clothes for your grandchildren that will provide years of enjoyment. Consider creating a permanent space for the storage of the dress-up items. A plastic bin or an old trunk work well. If you are fortunate enough to have an empty closet, put in some low hooks, a bin for storage, and a mirror on the wall. You can play dress-up right along with your grandchild. Be sure to have some odd items for Grandma: a funky hat, an old necktie, or a fancy scarf.

Let's Take a (Pretend) Vacation
3 years+

Supplies: Suitcases
            Dress-up clothes and accessories
            Construction paper
            Maps
            Two or three chairs
            Foreign coins, optional
            Expired passport, optional

With your grandchild, pick a vacation destination. Create tickets for your pretend trip. Draw maps or use real ones. Pack a suitcase with the necessary items. Create a pretend plane, train, or bus by setting up chairs to serve as seats. Do anything you can think of to simulate a real journey. Stuffed animals or dolls can be extra "family members" to accompany your grandchild on her trip.

Caps for Sale, a Drama
3 years+

Supplies: *Caps for Sale* by Esphyr Slobodkina
                     As many hats as you can gather up

This delightful children's book readily lends itself to a drama, acted out by a group of grandchildren or by Grandma and her grandchild.

The peddler in the story wears a stack of caps as he strolls through the village shouting, "Caps for sale." While the peddler naps with the caps on his head, monkeys steal the caps. Your grandchild can re-enact the drama by playing the part of the peddler or the monkey. Grandma can play the opposite role.

Other children's stories and books lend themselves to drama. Some examples are "The Three Bears," "The Three Little Pigs, "Three Billy Goat's Gruff," or *George and Martha* by James Marshall.

To Market, To Market, to Buy a . . .
3 years+

Supplies: Empty, clean food containers
                     Play food, purchased at a toy store
                     Play money, both paper and coins
                     Play cash register, optional

Children love to play grocery store. You can incorporate any of the following activities: shopping from a list, adding up prices, making change with play money, bagging items, and taking the groceries "home" to begin pretend cooking projects.

Wishes and Dreams
4 years+

Supplies: Variety of catalogs
              Play money
              Ribbon
              White paper
              Glue
              Paper punch
              Cardstock, optional

Collect catalogs of toys, clothes, books, furniture, or gift items. Make a *Dream Book* by punching holes in sheets of paper and tying the pages together with ribbon. Make a cover with colored cardstock, if you wish. Give your grandchild $500 in play money to "spend" however he wishes in the catalogs you have collected. (You can use Monopoly money or you can make pretend bills out of colored paper.) Help your grandchild cut out pictures of what wonderful items he would buy with the money and glue them into his very own *Dream Book*.

Drama, Drama, Drama
4 years+

Supplies: Simple story ideas
              Finger puppets
              Hand puppets
              Small theater, if available

Using purchased puppets or handmade puppets of cloth, papier mâché, or paper bags, plan a simple theater production with your grandchild. She can make up a story; she can expand on a simple nursery rhyme; or she can dramatize a tale like "The Three Little Pigs."

A puppet theater adds to the fun. You can create a theater out of a cardboard box with shirred fabric on a dowel rod for the curtain.

The play can be presented to an audience, if the child chooses. You can expand the activity to include homemade tickets and refreshments.

Mini Charades II
5 years+

Supplies: Pencil
              Pieces of paper

Write down basic activities and names of objects, each on separate slips of paper. Examples of activities: swimming, golfing, taking a shower, and washing the dishes. Examples of objects: car, book, violin, and bowl.

Model the activity for your grandchild by selecting one slip of paper and acting it out while your grandchild tries to guess. Then take turns.

Grandma's Notes and Ideas

What to Read?
Newborn+

Supplies: *The Read-Aloud Handbook* by Jim Trelease
                     Children's books

Trelease's suggestions for read-aloud books provide a fabulous resource for grandparents. By visiting the library or the bookstore prior to your grandchild's visit, you can select some of Trelease's recommended books to have on hand or to give as gifts. Read, read, read at every opportunity.

Word Processor I, Baby Writes a Story
4 months+

Supplies: Computer word-processing program

                     Printer with paper

A very young child can sit on Grandma's lap and watch letters and numbers appear on a computer screen. Grandma can make this activity more interesting and interactive by setting up the page with a huge font. As the child accidentally, and then purposefully, strikes the keyboard, Grandma can scroll the screen up and down so the child can view his work.

Print out the "story." Even the sound of the printer is entertaining.

Good Night Moon Game
6 months+

Supplies: *Goodnight Moon* by Margaret Wise Brown

Read *Goodnight Moon* to your grandchild before bedtime or nap time. Then on the way to her bedroom, say good night to everything you pass by.

Baby Faces
6 months+

Supplies: Small plastic photo album with clear sleeves
                    Baby photos of family members

Babies love other babies. Make your grandchild an album of her very own with family baby photos. Dig out those old photographs of your children or other family members when they were small. Enlarge them for a close-up of the face and cut to fit the photo album pages. As a surprise, include a photo of your grandchild and of your pets. For older babies and toddlers, you can use the photos as a starting place for family stories.

Is It Here Yet?
12 months+

Supplies: Subscription to an age-appropriate magazine

A subscription to a magazine is a treat. Children's magazines are full of stories, games, and craft ideas. Examples of magazines are Cricket's *Babybug* (1–3 years); Cricket's *Ladybug* (2–6 years); *Your Big Backyard* (3–7 years); *The American Girl Magazine* (7–10 years); *Cricket* (8–12 years).

Your grandchild can enjoy the magazine with you or on his own and feel very special that this treat is always waiting at Grandma's house. Long-distance Grandmas can send a subscription to the grandchild's home.

Rhyme Time
18 months–4 years

Supplies: Mother Goose book

Jump start your memory for nursery rhymes by checking out a Mother Goose book from the library. Learn a few rhymes by heart and recite them to your grandchild when the spirit moves you. Expand the fun by saying several rhyming words: sink, pink, mink. Encourage your grandchild to rhyme by saying, "What else rhymes with sink?" She may offer real words or made-up words. There will soon be many wiggles and giggles.

Tell Me a Story I
3 years+

Supplies: Willingness to listen
                 Imagination

Grandma can make up a story about anything at all. Your story might incorporate activities that have recently been part of the child's experience. The characters in your story might be children or animals familiar to your grandchild. Your story could document a day in the life of your grandchild's favorite toy. Let your imagination soar.

The logical evolution of "Tell Me a Story" is that your grandchild begins creating tales and sharing them with you. With encouragement, the child will have fun entertaining you and developing his imagination and storytelling skills.

Tell Me a Story II
3 years+

Supplies: Willingness to listen
                    Imagination

Another version of storytelling is "chain stories," in which Grandma begins the story, continues for several sentences, and then suddenly stops. Your grandchild then continues the same story until he decides to stop. Then the story goes back to Grandma for another turn. The only real problem with chain stories is deciding when the story is over. This activity can incorporate different ages at the same time.

Lost
3 years+

Supplies: Crayon or marker
                    Sticky notes

Depending on the age of your grandchild, write letters or words or sentences, one on each sticky note. Hide the sticky notes. Send your grandchild on a treasure hunt. You can say, "Six words are lost. See if you can find them." As your grandchild brings you a sticky note, you can encourage him to read the "lost" letters, words, or sentences.

Climb the Family Tree
3 years+

Supplies: Foam core board
Family photos
Glue stick
Your memory

Make copies of family photos. Cut out the faces. Draw a simple tree with branches on the foam core board. Glue the photos of each family member in place at the end of a branch, placing your grandchild's photo at the top center. Children can help with drawing the tree and gluing on the photos.

Tell your grandchild family stories. "The first time I saw you, I...." "When your mother was five, she...." You can involve the other grandparents in the planning of the family tree by asking them to share their family photos.

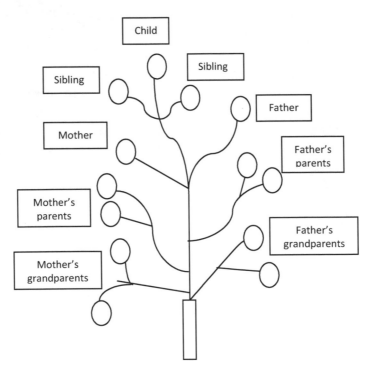

Word Processor II, Child Dictates a Story
4 years+

Supplies: Computer word-processing program
                         Printer with paper
                         A grandma typist

Encourage your grandchild to make up a story. Type up the story as the child tells it. (An older child may wish to type up the story himself.) Then print the story for reading aloud and for sharing with a parent or other person loved by the child.

Your grandchild can expand on the story at another time, if desired. He may wish, with your encouragement, to illustrate his story and add a cover.

Grandma can provide examples of books that have an introduction, a dedication, and an author biography. Encourage the child to add these features to his story.

A Whole New World of Books
4 years+

Supplies: Transportation to the public library

It is exciting to introduce a child to the public library. Grandma can call ahead to ask what the procedure is for a child to obtain a library card. A visiting grandchild should be able to check out books for the duration of her visit.

Who's Averse to Verse?
5 years+

Supplies: Books of poems for children
Imagination, interest, willingness to try
Paper
Tape recorder or video recorder, optional

Read aloud some simple poems. Suggested resources are: *Where the Sidewalk Ends* or *A Light in the Attic* both by Shel Silverstein; *The Random House Book of Poetry for Children* by Jack Prelutsky and Arnold Lobel; or a Mother Goose book. Repeat some rhyming words from the poetry to illustrate what a rhyme is.

Any of the following activities can be written down and read aloud to others, tape-recorded, or video-taped.

Create a list of rhyming words. For example, say to your grandchild, "What rhymes with 'pool?'" He might suggest the words cool, mule, stool, rule. Write down his words to use later in creating original poetry.

Make up verses to a familiar poem or song. For example:

> Old Mother Hubbard went to the cupboard
> To fetch her poor dog a bone.
> But when she got there, *there was nothing to share*
> *And the dog could do nothing but groan.*

Suggest that your grandchild create an original poem. He might write a verse about a particular special event or object. To get the ball rolling, Grandma can begin with a first line.

Two excellent resources for helping children write poetry are *Wishes, Lies, and Dreams* and *Rose, Where Did You Get That Red*, both by Kenneth Koch.

Round Robin Letters
5 years+

Supplies: Nice stationery
                  Pen, pencil, or other writing tool
                  Envelopes
                  First-class stamps

Everyone loves receiving mail. Send your grandchild (even if she lives in town) an age-appropriate, simple letter. Ask questions to invite responses. Even a brief "questionnaire" is appropriate, so she can fill in what she wants to say. Include a stamped, self-addressed envelope to encourage a return.

Grandma's Notes and Ideas

Scenes from the Stroller
Newborn–12 months

Supplies: Baby stroller

There are times when Grandma has to do her chores. There are times when Grandma's baby-toting muscles just won't cooperate. Bring the stroller inside the house. Buckle the baby in and give him a ride to the location of your next job.

For example, if you have laundry to fold, wheel him to the laundry room and make a show of folding each item, talking all the while. Make breezes on the baby as you shake out each item. Present a small item of clothing to the baby, take it away, and give it back. Baby will find you very entertaining.

Daisy, Daisy . . .
2 months–10 years

Supplies: Helmets
                             Bicycle for Grandma
                             Equipment appropriate for the age of the child

The experienced biking Grandma can share safe biking with her grandchild.

Specialized equipment, available to be rented or purchased at bike shops, is based on the child's age. Use your local bike shop for advice. The biking equipment options are:

- A cart attached to the back of Grandma's bike. The child rides inside; Grandma does the pedaling.
- A molded seat designed to fit on the back of Grandma's bike. The child is safely strapped in.
- A "co-pilot," a contraption with pedals and one tire that attaches to the back of Grandma's bike. This is for age 4 and older.
- A tandem bicycle.
- Two bicycles. Grandma guides and rides behind the child.

Bike to a destination: a friend's home, a restaurant, or a store. Bike on paved trails. Take water and snacks for a "picnic."

Babycizes
3-6 months

Supplies: Time and imagination

A few silly exercises with your grandchild can enliven diaper changes or add interest to play time.

- Bicycle baby's legs and say, "Run, run, run."
- Touch baby's hand to her opposite foot, making sizzling noises (b-zzz-t) when they touch. Do the other side.
- Gently push baby's knees into her belly, and say, "Gas Gone."
- Raise baby's arms and say, "Touchdown." Eventually you can teach the baby to raise her arms when you say the word. If the parents are sports fanatics, they will love your effort.

Baby Volunteers
3 months+

Supplies: Transportation
                   Arrangement with a local nursing home

Persons who reside in nursing homes or in assisted-living apartments love company, especially the company of babies. Telephone a nearby senior residence to see if they would welcome a visit. Arrange a specific time to visit there with your grandchild.

Consider organizing a group of babies and their accompanying grandmas to visit the facility on a regular basis. The group of adults and babies can sit in a circle near the residents and sing songs with simple actions like "If You're Happy and You Know It, Clap Your Hands" or "Head, Shoulders, Knees and Toes." Everybody wins in this time of sharing.

Baskets of Goodies
6 months–18 months

Supplies: Large baskets or other unbreakable containers
Any items you have around the house

Babies delight in manipulating objects. Strategically place baskets around the house, each filled with different household objects or a combination of objects to discover. Ideas include pinecones, wooden spoons, measuring cups, plastic containers, junk mail, catalogs, metal bowls with metal spoons.

Box Car
6 months+

Supplies: Cardboard box or a sturdy
plastic laundry basket

When your grandchild can sit on her own, place her in the box and push her around the room, tossing in toys as you go.

Grandma's Purse
6 months+

Supplies: Large, empty handbag

                    Age-appropriate objects

Purses are fun to explore. Fill a large handbag with goodies of all kinds. Bring the purse with you when you visit your grandchild or have it available when she visits you.

For babies who are still mouthing everything, select plastic keys, an old handkerchief, teething biscuits, stacking cups, teething rings, and a toy cell phone.

For older children select a big old wallet, an old set of real keys, a Kleenex package (you can purchase fancy, patterned ones), money, some candy, flavored lip balm, a mirror, an old cell phone, and an old calculator.

Scarf Fun
6 months+

Supplies: Lightweight scarves

Select several scarves in a variety of colors, patterns, and textures. You can:

- Toss a scarf into the air. As it floats down, catch it in your arms.
- Tell your grandchild to hold out his arms. Toss another scarf for him to catch.
- Talk about the colors of the scarves.
- Wad the scarves into balls and toss them to your grandchild.
- Play peek-a-boo with the scarves.
- Dance to music with the scarves.
- Play dress-up making a scarf skirt, belt, or hat.

Where is Baby's Shin?
9 months+

Supplies: Purchased circle or star stickers

To play the game, you can:

- Call out the names of parts of the body and place a sticker on the spot.
- Call out the names to see if your grandchild can point to the correct spot. Place a sticker.
- Call out the names to see if your grandchild can point to the correct spot on Grandma. Place a sticker.

If your grandchild can identify many common parts of the body, you can teach more difficult ones like shin and elbow.

Did You Hear That?
6 months–2 years

Supplies: Large mailbox

While you are out on a walk, stop at your mailbox. Lift up your grandchild, open the door, and shout inside. Did you hear the echo? Take turns yelling or singing a song into the mailbox.

Tunnel Fun
8 months–3 years

Supplies: Large boxes

Make a tunnel out of a large wardrobe box or tape several open-ended boxes together for your grandchild to crawl through.

It's Stuck
9-18 months

Supplies: Duct tape
Small objects
Piece of contact paper about two-feet long

Tape the contact paper to the floor sticky side up. Peel off the backing. Place objects such as a baby spoon, masking tape roll, or small toys on the contact paper. Help the child lift the objects off the sticky paper. Place your grandchild's hand or foot on the sticky paper. Explore the concepts sticky, stuck, and unstuck.

Cardboard Creativity I
9 months+

Supplies: Cardboard tubes from toilet paper
Cardboard tubes from paper towels
Empty tissue boxes

Recycle cardboard household items for the enjoyment of your grandchild. A very young child will laugh as Grandma sings or talks to her through the cardboard tube. You can look at the baby through the tube and have the baby look through the tube at you and then at other objects. An empty paper towel tube is great for drumming, banging, or swatting at a hanging object. An empty tissue box is perfect for collecting objects. Your grandchild can shake box to enjoy the sound. She can retrieve the objects and put them back in the box again.

Kiddie Kisses
9 months+

Supplies:　　　Grandma and her grandchild

Teach your grandchild to blow a kiss. Once he learns this skill you can blow kisses to each other, to dolls, to stuffed animals, and to your reflections in the mirror.

Here Comes the Bag Lady
9 months+

Supplies:　　　Large, heavy-duty tote bag
　　　　　　　Age-appropriate projects

When you are going to visit your grandchild, plan projects for the two of you to do together: paper dolls, art projects, yarn projects, puzzles, or activities from this book. Use a baggie for the supplies and directions for each project. Fill your tote bag with the projects. Take your Grandma Bag with you every time you visit your grandchild. He will quickly learn to anticipate the arrival of Grandma and her projects.

Fort Fun
9 months+

Supplies: Blankets or sheets
Table or chairs
Pillows or cushions

Spread a blanket over a table or the backs of chairs to make a fort. With the fort, you can:

- Play hide and seek or peek-a-boo.
- Have a snack inside.
- Read a book inside.
- Take a nap inside.

Create an elaborate structure for pretend camping. Sofa cushions make good beds inside the tent.

Cardboard Creativity II
12 months–18 months

Supplies: Shoe box
Cardboard tubes from toilet paper

Make a box that your grandchild can push objects into. Cut three holes slightly larger than the diameter of the tube in the lid of a shoe box. Cut the tube in half or in thirds so that your grandchild can push the cardboard pieces into the box. Shake the box, open it, and let your grandchild pull the pieces out and push them back in again. She may enjoy pushing other objects or toys into the holes.

Growth Ladder
12 months+

Supplies: Blank wall
                Pencil
                Yardstick or tape measure

Select a wall behind a door or in any out-of-the-way location. Keep a growth record of your grandchild so you can both be amazed at her progress. Mark the child's height on the wall with a pencil each time she visits (or occasionally, if she's there often). Write the date and the height next to the line. Keep a "ladder" for each grandchild.

Bean Bag Bounty
15 months+

Supplies: Felt squares of several different colors
Sewing machine
Purchased dried beans
Needle and thread, optional

Purchase felt squares from a local craft or discount store. Cut felt into three- or four-inch squares. Sew up three sides with the sewing machine. Fill the beanbags with dried beans and stitch the end closed. These beanbags have multiple uses, some of which will come from the creativity of your grandchild.

- Beanbags can be stacked into towers and knocked over.
- Beanbags can become pillows for dolls or stuffed animals.
- Beanbags can be used to learn colors and directions. "Bring me the purple beanbag." "Take the yellow beanbag over to the rocking chair."
- Beanbags can be tossed at a specific target, like a towel hanging from a chair.
- Beanbags can be tossed into a wastebasket for a game. An older child will enjoy keeping score.

Blanket Ride
18 months-2½ years

Supplies: Large blanket or towel

Place your grandchild in the middle of a large blanket and drag him slowly around the floor. Go fast. Go slow. Ask your grandchild to give you directions about speed and when to stop. If your grandchild is reluctant, try this activity with a doll or stuffed animal.

Bottle Bowling
2-5 years

Supplies: Empty plastic bottles
                Big rubber ball

Set up the plastic bottles and see how many your grandchild can bowl down by rolling the ball toward the bottles. Repeat. Repeat. Repeat.

Field Trips Galore
2-10 years

Supplies: Automobile
Car seat appropriate for age of the child
Grandma's cash stash, depending on activity

Field trips come in many shapes and sizes. Here are some ideas for field trips: nature center, children's museum, music store, fire station, farm with animals, pet store, nearby historical markers, manufacturing plant, pumpkin patch, turkey farm, construction site, skateboard park, doggie park (you don't need a dog), recycling center, thrift store (like Goodwill), apple orchard, Christmas tree farm, jewelry store, tide pools, Grandpa's work, or a dollar store. If necessary, phone ahead to check on hours.

Think creatively. What about searching for the end of a rainbow (if you are lucky enough to see one)? How far is it to the grain silo or skyscraper? Everyone gets a guess and you can drive there to find out the real distance. How many squirrels will you see on your walk in the woods? Count them as you walk.

Coin Toss
2½-10 years

Supplies: Lots of coins

                   Unmowed or woodsy area in your yard

Is Grandma tired? Here's an idea for your grandchild while you lounge on an outdoor chair. Without your grandchild's knowledge, go outside and toss a bunch of coins around in an area you don't mow. Then send your grandchild on a hunt for coins. Whatever she finds she may keep. You might tell an older child exactly how much money is "hidden" and have her count up her find.

An alternative activity is to hide coins indoors for your grandchild to find and to deposit in her piggy bank.

Casino Delight
2½ years+

Supplies: Large quantity of poker chips

Devise simple poker chip games. You can toss the chips into a wastebasket. You can throw the chips beyond a certain line. You can stack the chips until they fall. You can sort the chips by color.

For an older grandchild, you can add numerical value to the chips and practice addition. At a later age, play poker for real.

Magical Mystery Ride
2½ years+

Supplies: A car
                      Scarf for a blindfold

Buckle your grandchild into his car seat. Blindfold him and take him on a special trip, all the while asking him if he can guess where you are going. Your destination and the length of the ride will depend on the age of your grandchild. Ideas for a special destination are an ice cream store, a book store, a playground, a toy store, the library for story time, or a movie theater for a children's matinee.

Gone Fishing
3 years+

Supplies: Yardstick
                      Heavy string or twine
                      Circular magnet with a center hole
                      Paperclips
                      Large, plastic tray, optional
                      Construction paper, optional

"Go fishing" indoors. The yardstick is the fishing pole, the magnet is the hook, and the paperclips are the fish.

Thread one end of a long piece of string through the hole of the magnet and secure the string with a knot. Tie the other end of the string to the yardstick. Spread the paperclip fish on the floor or on a large plastic tray. Your grandchild casts his line into the pool to catch the fish.

If you choose to be more elaborate, cut fish out of construction paper and attach the paperclips to these fish.

Obstacle Course
3-10 years

Supplies: Household items

Stop watch, optional

Design a simple obstacle course with a few stations for your grandchild to conquer. Following is an example of an obstacle course.

Station 1:   Toss a bean bag into a wastebasket.

Station 2:   Crawl under a row of chair legs.

Station 3:   Jump up and down 10 times.

Station 4:   Bounce and catch a ball 5 times.

Your grandchild proceeds from one station to the next until he completes the course.

For a younger child, begin with only two very simple activities. Grandma can complete the course herself and then encourage the child to try. At each station Grandma calls out the directions for the child to follow.

For an older child, write out the directions and place them at each station. Your grandchild may wish to do timed runs, may challenge Grandma to a timed contest, or may add more stations to the course.

Button, Button, Who's Got the Button
3 years+

Supplies: A variety of buttons

Most Grandmas have a good collection of buttons. Put the buttons into a container with a lid that the child can open herself. The following are some button possibilities:

- Make buttons into pretend food for a tea party.
- Sort buttons by color type, size, or "favorites."
- String buttons on a string or shoelace for a necklace.
- Buy a T-shirt and decorate the front with buttons. With Grandma's help, the older child can learn the skill of attaching a button to an article of clothing.

Talent Show
3 years+

Supplies: Several children
       Costumes, props, and music

Most children enjoy performing. Channel this enthusiasm into a talent show. Grandma may need to help with organization. Each child can choose a type of performance: a song, a poem, a dance, a drawing, or a dramatic presentation with another child. Encourage him to practice his talent in preparation for the performance.

An older child, or Grandma, can be the Mistress of Ceremonies and make elaborate introductions. The other performers can serve as the audience. Videotaping the performances is optional.

Special treats can follow the performance.

Treasure Hunt I
3 years+

Supplies: Grandma
             Prizes (toy, food, book, gift certificate)

Treasure hunts can take place indoors or out. Before your grandchild arrives, place written clues around the house. These clues direct your grandchild to one clue after another and finally to the prize.

For the pre-reader, picture drawings can show where to go next or Grandma can read the clues. For the reader, Grandma can write out simple directions for the child to read herself.

Where Am I?
3 years+

Supplies: Bandana or large cloth for a blindfold

Blindfold your grandchild. Lead him around the house or around the outside, asking him to guess where he is. Give him objects to feel, seeing if he can identify them.

Reverse roles: blindfold yourself, take a deep breath, and allow your grandchild lead you around.

Treasure Hunt II
3 years+

Supplies: Prizes
                     Ball of thick yarn

Establish a starting point. Prepare the activity ahead of time. Unwind the yarn over, under, around, and through many rooms and objects in the house until reaching a spot where a prize is tied to the end of the yarn. Your grandchild, beginning at the starting point, follows the yarn around all the obstacles to reach the prize.

This activity can be simple or very complicated, going up and down stairs, around door knobs, over and under furniture.

To set up the hunt for several children, use a different color of yarn for each child.

Frank Lloyd Wright
3 years+

Supplies: Cardboard boxes
                     Packing tape
                     Tempera paints, crayons, or markers

Find the largest box you can. A grocery store or a moving company is a good source. Cut windows (Grandma does this part) and use the open end as a door. Your grandchild can paint or decorate the exterior of the box. The child's artwork or some fabric scraps can decorate the interior. The box can be taped to other boxes and an entire building or town can be created. This is a large, space-consuming activity that can last for months. Your grandchild may never want to take it apart. The older the child, the more imaginative she will be in creating her own space for reading, napping, and playing games.

Are We There Yet? I
3 years+

Supplies: A car trip

                Recognition skills for letters of the alphabet

Young children can pass the time on a car trip with the fun of alphabet recognition. Begin with the first letter of the alphabet and find an "A" on road and highway signs. Next look on subsequent signs for a "B." You can go through the alphabet as many times as the children remain interested.

Shadow Play
3-10 years

Supplies: Two hands

                Source of light (flashlight or bare light bulb)

                Light-colored wall

Remember hand shadows, the animals you create by manipulating your hands in front of a light source? Take some time to learn a few simple positions like the giraffe, the swan, and the rabbit. *The Art of Hand Shadows* by Albert Almoznino illustrates dozens of shadows. Young children can enjoy making shadows of their stuffed animals or dolls. Children of many ages love to perform as a shadow. Sun shadows are fun to chase.

Movie Night
3-10 years

Supplies: Child-appropriate movie, rented or purchased
              Popcorn, candy, beverages

Spread pillows and blankets on the floor in front of your TV. Make popcorn and put it into purchased cardboard popcorn containers. Provide drinks and other treats. Discuss the movie afterwards. Include a sleepover for your grandchild and a friend, if you're up to it.

Marvelous Miniatures
3-10 years

Supplies: Small boxes
              Paper cups
              Cardboard tubes from toilet paper
              Cardboard tubes from paper towels
              Glue and paint, optional

Think small. Think creatively. Gather a variety of small cardboard items. Look at the shapes and imagine what you can make. Some possibilities are: a miniature town, including a church, a post office, and skyscrapers; a farmstead, including barns and silos; the grandchild's neighborhood, including houses, a grocery store, and a gas station. Painting the boxes and gluing them together to build larger structures can be part of this activity.

Heads or Tails
4-10 years

Supplies: A coin

A stroll through Grandma's neighborhood can turn into an adventure. At the first intersection, flip a coin. If it lands on heads, turn left; if it lands on tails, turn right. At the next intersection, flip the coin again. Continue in this manner until one of you tires of the coin-directed stroll. Race back home.

Pig Latin and Other Secrets
5 years+

Supplies: Paper and pencil
                        Internet for research, optional

Big kids and little kids love secrets.

- Teach your grandchild Pig Latin. Rammagay oveslay ouyay means Grandma loves you.
- Teach your grandchild Morse code.
- Create a code with your grandchild.
- Develop a secret handshake.

Any of these ideas can be the secret means of communication between you and your grandchild.

Talent Share with Grandma
5 years+

Supplies: Grandma's talent
             Items related to your talent

Every Grandma has special talents, interests, or skills. Do you play the piano, crochet, collect stamps or coins, paint or draw? Do you sing, sew, garden, jog, dance, cook, photograph, scrapbook? Identify your talent and share it with your grandchild.

Let's say that your talent is tap dancing. Drag out your old tap shoes and demonstrate a tap dance. Purchase a pair of used, child-sized tap shoes at a local dance supply store and teach your grandchild one or two easy steps.

Depending on your grandchild's interest in your talent, teach more difficult skills. Then you can turn the tables for your grandchild's next visit and ask him to prepare to teach you a talent.

Back Seat Driver
5-10 years

Supplies: A car
             Pencil and paper

Take a child-directed trip to the country. Ask your grandchild to tell you when or where to turn. An older grandchild can write down the directions in order to reverse them for the trip home.

When your trip is finished, discuss the sights you've seen.

A, B, C, D
6 years+

Supplies: Phonebook
                  Index cards

Children like to learn how the alphabet is useful. Write a few easy last names (Smith, Green) on index cards for your grandchild to read. Have her look up the name in the phonebook. She can count how many Smiths live in your town. This is an entertaining game for a car trip.

Are We There Yet? II
6 years+

Supplies: A car trip, a restaurant, or a rainy day

The first person states a geographical name such as a city, a country, or a river. The next person then states another geographical word, but it must *begin* with the *last* letter of the word in the preceding turn. Example: England, then Denver, then Rhode Island. This game can go on for quite a long time. Older children can help the younger ones.

Merlin the Magician
8 years+

Supplies: Book of magic tricks

There are many "how to" books of magic tricks on the market. Select an age-appropriate book with good illustrations to have on hand for your grandchild's visit. An excellent book is *Card Tricks – 30 Easy to Follow Tricks to Amaze Your Family and Friends* by James Weir. Magic trick props such as a black hat or a magic wand are available for purchase at toy or craft stores.

The child can select and practice his magic tricks and be pleased with his progress and expertise. He can develop a "show" for an audience. He can add running commentary, tickets, and treats.

Grandma's Notes and Ideas

Animal Delights
12 months+

Supplies: Nature calendar with animal photos
8 ½ x 11-inch plastic sleeves
Three-ring binder

Wildlife organizations publish yearly calendars. Often the calendar photos are of animals and their babies, a fascination to any small child. He can learn their names and identify the mama and her baby.

Choose some calendar photos for a book for your grandchild. Place the pages in plastic sleeves to protect them and insert the pages in a three-ring binder. You and your grandchild have created *Animal Delights,* a book to be discussed and expanded.

Abstract Art
12 months–2 years

Supplies: Paper towel or white paper coffee filters
                      Washable markers
                      Masking tape

Place your grandchild in her highchair. Use masking tape to secure the paper towel or coffee filter to the tray. Encourage her to draw with the markers. The paper absorbs the ink from the markers, and the colors blur into abstract art.

Never Fail Play Clay
18 months–4 years

Supplies: 2 cups flour
                      1/2 cup salt
                      2 cups water
                      2 tablespoons oil
                      1/4 cup cream of tartar
                      1-3 T food coloring

Mix the first 5 ingredients in a saucepan. Add food coloring and stir well. Cook the dough over medium-low heat until a ball is formed and the dough is no longer sticky. Allow to cool slightly before storing in an air tight container. (For two colors of play clay, cook the dough in two batches, adding a different color to each.)

Show your grandchild the fun of rolling snakes between her palms. Encourage her to sculpt an imaginary critter. Flatten the play clay and cut out shapes with small cookie cutters.

Paper Bag People
18 months–3 years

Supplies: Newspaper or old catalogs
                         Lunch sack or paper bag
                         Rubber band
                         Crayons, markers, or paint

Provide lots of newspaper or catalogs for your grandchild to tear up, crumple and stuff into the paper bag. When the bag is full, help him close the end with a rubber band. Draw a face on the bag.

Picasso Grande
2-4 years

Supplies: Several pieces of paper taped together
                         Crayons or washable markers
                         Masking tape

Tape the large sheets of paper to the floor. Encourage your grandchild to draw all over the paper by moving around as needed. Grandma can draw on her own piece of paper or draw on the same paper as her grandchild.

Sandpaper Design
2-4 years

Supplies: Coarse sandpaper
                         Yarn pieces in a variety of colors

Coarse sandpaper and yarn can be combined to make a work of art. Cut yarn into varying lengths. Show your grandchild how to press a yarn piece to the sandpaper until it sticks. Encourage him to continue adding yarn to make a unique design.

Sun Catchers
2-5 years

Supplies: Clear contact paper
Brightly colored tissue paper
Scissors
Paper punch
Piece of yarn

Cut colored tissue paper into simple shapes of varying sizes. Cut out two identical squares of clear contact paper. Peel the backing off one square and place it, sticky side up, on a table, securing the square with tape. Allow your grandchild to drop, place, pat or throw the tissue paper shapes onto the contact paper.

When he is finished making his design, peel the backing off the second piece of contact paper and smooth it down on his decorated piece. Punch a hole at the top and thread a piece of yarn through for hanging in a sunny window.

Puppets Galore
2-5 years

Supplies: Cardboard tubes from paper towels
Cardboard tubes from toilet paper
Markers or crayons
Fabric scraps
Yarn

Make a puppet or a family of puppets from empty cardboard tubes. With markers, draw a face on one end of the tube. Glue on yarn for hair. Dress the puppet with stickers or scraps of lace and fabric. Use the other end of the tube to hold the puppet and to move it about for make-believe play.

Rock On!
2½-10 years

Supplies: Rocks
                   Tempera or acrylic paint
                   Paintbrush

Take a walk with your grandchild, collecting smooth rocks in a variety of shapes and sizes. Wash and dry the rocks. Your grandchild can paint the rocks as critters, as people, or with designs. Each child will create a unique art piece that can be given to her parents as a paperweight or set on Grandma's shelf for a decoration.

T-Shirts, Painted
2½-10 years

Supplies: 100% cotton T-shirt
                   Cloth paints

Your grandchild can paint on cotton T-shirts with specialized cloth paints, available at craft or discount stores. She can use a brush or her hands to paint a design. Another option is to dip the child's hand in the paint and place her prints on a shirt or sweatshirt. Grandma can help write the child's name next to the handprint.

Your grandchild may choose to paint on any item of 100% cotton fabric such as an apron, a dishtowel, a purse, or a scarf.

Jewels I
3 years+

Supplies: Uncooked pasta pieces with holes
Yarn, string, elastic cord or shoelaces
Tempera paints
Large plastic needle

Create a necklace or bracelet from uncooked pasta. Pasta that is about one-inch long, slightly curved and hollow works well for this activity. Your grandchild will enjoy painting the pieces different colors, letting them dry, and then stringing them for gifts. Wrapping the gift can be part of the activity.

Froot Loop Sand Painting
3-7 years

Supplies: Froot Loops cereal
Food processor or rolling pin
Plastic baggie
Construction paper
Glue stick or white glue

Use a rolling pin to crush Froot Loops cereal in a sealed plastic baggie. (To make finer-textured sand, use a food processor.) Have your grandchild rub the glue stick (or spread the glue) in a design on a piece of construction paper. Sprinkle the Froot Loop sand onto the glue. For ease of sprinkling the sand, you can use a clean spice bottle with a shaker top or a Parmesan cheese shaker.

T-Shirts, Personalized
3 years+

Supplies: Cotton T-shirt
                       Ink-jet T-shirt transfer paper
                       Computer word-processing program

Grandchildren get a huge kick out of creating personalized clothing. Grandma can help create a T-shirt with the child's name, the child's photo, or a message like "Happy Birthday, Dad."

Purchase specialized T-shirt transfer paper at an office supply store. Create a design for the T-shirt in a word-processing program, enlarging or enhancing in any way you wish. Print the image on the transfer paper. Iron the transfer onto the front of the T-shirt according to the directions that accompany the transfer paper.

Tips for a successful T-shirt experience:

- Practice creating a design before your grandchild arrives.
- Download several choices of free clip art from the Internet that your grandchild might enjoy. Have the clip art readily available on your computer desktop.
- You might also pre-select family photos from your computer files as possible T-shirt choices.
- To create a mirror image of a caption you can write your message in WordArt on Microsoft Word and flip your message horizontally. Print it out on plain paper and check your results in a mirror to see if it's what you expected.
- In the *properties* of some printers, you can select *mirror image* to print out your message.

Puzzled?
3 years+

Supplies: White poster board
Poster paints, markers, or crayons
Scissors

Encourage your grandchild to draw or paint a picture on a piece of poster board. After the picture is dry, turn it over and with a pencil, draw puzzle-shaped pieces. (Grandma can help with this.) Cut apart the pieces. Take turns putting the puzzle together. Store the puzzle in an envelope or a plastic bag for later use.

A younger child can select a picture from a magazine and glue it on a piece of cardboard for her puzzle. Grandma can cut the picture into large puzzle pieces.

Hmmmm! Scent!
3 years+

Supplies: Large oranges
Lots of whole cloves
Ribbon
Straight pins

Help your grandchild press the sharp end of whole cloves into an orange. Continue until the orange is covered. With straight pins tack ribbon around the orange. Make a loop for hanging at the top and then tie a bow. The clove-citrus sachet adds a nice scent to a closet, a drawer, or the kitchen.

Chained In
3 years+

Supplies: Colored construction paper
                    Ruler
                    Scissors
                    Glue or glue stick

Share the joy of paper chains with your grandchild. For the younger age group, Grandma can pre-cut strips of the colored paper to measure about 1 inch by 8 ½ inches. Your grandchild will love gluing the strips into intertwining circles.

An older grandchild can draw around all sides of a ruler on sheets of colored paper, creating long, narrow strips to cut out. Encourage him to cut strips of various lengths, colors, and widths. He can decorate his strips with glitter and sequins before gluing them together.

Soap on a Rope
3 years+

Supplies: Plastic or fabric rope
                    Electric drill
                    Soap

Soap on a rope hangs around your neck so the soap doesn't slip, fall, or get lost while you lather up in the shower.

Using an electric drill, make a hole through the center of the soap while your grandchild "supervises." Then the child can thread the rope through the hole and tie the ends in a knot or bow. (The length of the rope is determined by who the recipient of the soap will be.)

Kodak Moments
3 years+

Supplies: Simple digital camera
Small photo album

From the age of 3, a child can look through and click a digital camera to take a photo. As his camera skills improve, he will learn to center the picture and to focus.

Print the pictures on a home printer or upload to a local drugstore for printing. You can make an album of a vacation trip, a Grandma visit, or any other event.

For an older child, the skills of editing and cropping can be introduced, using computer software or the photo machines at the drugstore.

Stepping Stones
3 years+

Supplies: Concrete powder
Plastic ice cream container for mixing
Shallow, plastic container for a mold

The easiest method to create a stepping stone for the garden is to purchase a kit at a craft store. The least expensive method is to buy a small bag of concrete powder at a local hardware store or lumber yard.

Mix a small amount of concrete powder as directed. Pour it into the mold to a depth of about two inches. When the mixture begins to stiffen, your grandchild can then press her palm print, her footprint, rocks, jewels, or other sturdy items into the cement. She can also inscribe her name. The piece, when hardened and unmolded, makes a treasured gift for a parent or grandparent.

Pasta Collage
3 years+

Supplies: Pasta in a variety of shapes
White glue
Heavy cardboard
Acrylic paints

Your grandchild can make an interesting collage by gluing pasta shapes onto the cardboard. When the collage is dry, he can paint his creation.

Veggie Collage
3 years+

Supplies: Dried peas, beans, corn, lentils
White glue
Heavy cardboard
Acrylic or poster paints, optional

Begin the collage by having your grandchild paint the cardboard, if desired. Allow to dry. Your grandchild can glue the dried beans, peas, corn and lentils on the cardboard to create a colorful and unique work of art.

Thanksgiving Turkey Hand
3 years+

Supplies: Large piece of white paper
Crayons, markers, a pencil
Feathers, yarn, other decorative objects

Place your grandchild's hand on the paper and carefully draw around it with a pencil. This hand outline will become a Thanksgiving turkey The thumb is the turkey's head; the other four fingers are the turkey's plumage. Your grandchild can decorate the turkey by adding eyes or a wattle. He can color in the tail feathers or decorate them with yarn or purchased feathers. He can make an entire family of turkeys.

Total Body Portrait
3 years+

Supplies: Large paper or several pieces taped together
Pencil
Crayons or markers

Tape a sheet of paper to the floor that is large enough to draw around the child's body. Have the child lie down on the paper, face up, with arms out slightly from her sides. Draw around the child from head to toe. When finished, let the child get up and see how big she is. Then she can color her figure in any way she chooses, adding clothes, facial features, and hair. You can reverse this and have your grandchild draw Grandma, but you'll need larger paper!

Easy Christmas Crafts I
3-10 years

Supplies: Popped corn
                 Cranberries
                 Needle
                 Heavy thread

Thread the popped corn and berries in separate strands to make garlands for a Christmas tree. Ask younger children to hand you the berries to string. Older children will want to use the needle and thread themselves. Tell your grandchild about your Christmas traditions as you are stringing.

From Scrap to Sculpture
4-10 years

Supplies: Small pieces of scrap wood
                 Wood glue
                 Rectangle of wood for the base
                 Paint and paintbrushes

In this activity your grandchild fashions pieces of wood into a three-dimensional sculpture. Collect small pieces of scrap wood in varying sizes and shapes.

Your grandchild glues the pieces of wood on to the base rectangle in any way she chooses. As the sculpture evolves, it may grow to many layers before your grandchild declares that it is finished. The wood scraps may be painted before assembling or the finished sculpture may be painted in one color or in different colors. Some children prefer to leave the wood surfaces unfinished. Cardboard shapes, string, paper, buttons, or other scrap items may also be incorporated into the sculpture.

Easy Christmas Crafts II
4 years+

Supplies: Aluminum foil
Cardboard
Cookie cutters in Christmas shapes
Paper punch
Ribbon

Draw around a cookie cutter on sturdy cardboard. Cut out the shapes. Cover each shape with aluminum foil to catch the Christmas lights. Punch a hole near the top and thread in ribbon to make a hanger for the ornament.

If you can tolerate more mess, use white poster board for the shapes and decorate with glitter or pieces of ribbon.

Coasters Creations
4 years+

Supplies: Self-adhesive laminating sheets
Child's art work

Your grandchild can use his handprint, a photograph of himself, or a picture he has drawn to create coasters.

A simple coaster, for example, can be created from the child's handprint. First, draw around your grandchild's hand several times. He may color each handprint if he wishes. Next, laminate each handprint according to the package directions. Finally, cut the laminated designs into identical circles or squares for a set of coasters.

Finger Prints and Other Inking
4 years+

Supplies: Black stamp pad with washable ink
Commercially sold stamps
Markers, crayons, pastel oil crayons
Good quality paper

Stamp pads provide a variety of activities. The child can make greeting cards, wrapping paper, and other decorations by stamping designs on the paper. The stamped designs can be colored in, painted, or filled in with markers. A child can also use her own fingerprints to create designs on the paper.

Deck the Halls
4 years+

Supplies: Holiday decorations
Unlined file cards
Stickers
Plain or embossed napkins
Markers or crayons

Children enjoy decorating for any holiday. You and your grandchild can:

- Unpack your holiday-specific decorations and let your grandchild place them around the house.
- Make place cards for the holiday meal by using unlined file cards, folded in half. Write the name of a guest on each card. Your grandchild can decorate the place cards with yarn, fabric, ribbon, stickers, markers, or anything you have on hand. He will enjoy placing the cards on the table to choose where family members will sit.
- Add stickers to plain, white paper napkins to make them festive or color the embossed designs.

Remember that any day can be a holiday of your choosing. You can celebrate half birthdays, Sadie Hawkins' Day, or make up your own holiday.

Jewels II
4 years+

Supplies: Carrots
Radishes
Apple
Yarn, elastic cord, or jewelry cord
Large-eyed needle

Slice the carrots and radishes into thin disks. Peel the apple and cut into pieces. Air dry all the vegetable and fruit pieces overnight. As the pieces dry, they will form interesting shapes, similar to pieces of coral. Thread a needle with yarn, elastic cord, or jewelry cord and string the items into necklaces or bracelets. Your grandchild can make jewelry of all one type of "jewel" or mix the "jewels" on the cord.

Potato Prints
4 years+

Supplies: Large baking potato
Sharp knife
Pencil
Stamp pad
Paper

Cut off the end of the potato to reveal a flat surface. Dry off the moisture. Now your grandchild can pencil onto the potato a shape that he would like to print. A heart is a good shape to begin with.

Depending on the age of the child, Grandma or the child can cut away at the potato to make the heart stick out. Again, wipe away the moisture. Then use the potato as a stamper, inking it, and stamping the shape onto paper. Create designs, greeting cards, wrapping paper, or whatever your grandchild wishes.

Hanging Ornament
5 years+

Supplies: A small balloon
Yarn in various colors and thicknesses
White glue
Wax paper

Cover your work surface with wax paper. Blow up the balloon and secure it with a knot. Have the child saturate some lengths of yarn with white glue. Wrap the wet yarn all around the balloon to create a lacy design. After the yarn is dry, pop the balloon and remove it. This will become a hard, lightweight decoration that can be hung anywhere with thread, fish line, or additional yarn.

Animal Cracker Pins
5 years+

Supplies: Animal crackers
Purchased jewelry pin backs
White glue
Spray varnish

Each individual animal cracker has the potential to become a pin to wear. Glue a pin back to the smooth side of the animal cracker. Use a lot of white glue, creating a pool of it to hold the pin. Allow the glue to dry completely. With Grandma's supervision, your grandchild can varnish the front, back, and sides of the pin to keep it from crumbling. Grandma can wear the pin for a long time!

Snip, Snip
5-10 years

Supplies: Squares of white paper, any size
                     Child-sized scissors

Show your grandchild how to fold a square sheet of white paper in half and then in half again. Make snips and slits on the folds and on the edges for a unique snowflake. Use as window decorations.

Silhouettes on the Shade
5 years+

Supplies: Large sheet of white paper
                     Masking tape
                     Darkened room
                     Directional lamp
                     Pencil

Tape the paper to a wall. Sit your grandchild in a chair with his side facing the wall. Shine the lamp so his silhouette appears on the paper. Draw the child's face in profile, outlining nose, lips, shape of head, and even a quirky piece of hair. Grandma or the child can cut out the silhouette. Then reverse, having the child do Grandma's silhouette.

Jewels III
7 years+

Supplies: Jewelry discards
Buttons from Grandma's button box
Elastic cord for stringing necklaces or bracelets
Purchased wires for making earrings

Using scissors or small wire cutters, take apart some jewelry pieces. Your grandchild can lay out the buttons and jewels to decide on an arrangement. She can string the pieces together as a necklace or a bracelet or use the purchased wires to make earrings. She may wish to supplement the pieces with a few beads from a craft store. She can choose to wear her creation or gift it.

Knit One, Purl One
7-10 years

Supplies: Knitting needles about 8-inches long
Yarn
An instruction book with good drawings

Children are fascinated with the process of knitting. If you knit, share the knowledge and skill. Your grandchildren can practice the stitches and then make a simple scarf.

Excellent books for teaching children to knit are *Kids Knitting: Projects for Kids of All Ages* by Melanie Falick; *Kids' Easy Knitting Projects (Quick Starts for Kids!)* by Peg Blanchette; *Kids! Picture Yourself Knitting* by maranGraphics Development Group. These books also include age-appropriate knitting projects.

Taking your grandchild to the knitting store to select his yarn can be part of the activity.

Grandma's Notes and Ideas

Yummy Colors
2½-5 years

Supplies: 1 can white frosting
Food coloring – red, yellow and blue
Wax paper
3 bowls
3 spoons
Graham crackers, optional

Spoon a small amount frosting into each of three bowls. Add red food coloring to one bowl of frosting, blue to the second, and yellow to the third. Stir, stir, stir until all the frosting is colored. Let your grandchild mix two colors together on a piece of wax paper to see what color appears. Try all the color combinations. After you are finished with the experiment, spread the frosting on graham crackers for a snack. Then read the book *Mouse Paint* by Ellen Stoll Walsh.

Static
2½-10 years

Supplies: Empty soda pop can
              Balloon

Blow up a balloon.

- Set the soda can on its side on the floor. Rub the inflated balloon back and forth on your grandchild's hair. Hold the balloon close to, but not touching, one side of the can. As you move the balloon, the can will move.
- Have your grandchild stand in front of a mirror. Rub the balloon on your grandchild's hair and slowly pull it away. A new hair style!
- Turn on the faucet and run a trickle of water. Rub the balloon on your grandchild's hair and hold it near the water. The water will bend.

Younger children will be amazed. Older children can research protons and electrons on the Internet.

Bubble Action
3-6 years

Supplies: Raisins
              Carbonated water
              Tall, clear glass

Your grandchild can carefully pour the carbonated water into a glass. Then she can drop a few raisins into the water to see what will happen. The air bubbles will make the raisins rise and fall.

Will It Float?
3 years+

Supplies: Bucket or a sink
                     Household objects

Take a stroll around the house and the outdoors with your grandchild, collecting objects that won't be damaged by water, such as a rock, a bar of Ivory soap, a plastic cup, a penny.

Fill a bucket or a sink with water. Select one object and ask your grandchild, "Will it float?" Test the question by dropping the object into the water. Continue in the same manner with all the objects you have collected.

The Summer Sun
3-8 years

Supplies: A sunny day
                     Various flat objects
                     Dark construction paper

Ask your grandchild to search the house and yard for flat, solid objects. A rock, a playing card, a spoon, a ruler, and a key will work well for this activity. Place a sheet of construction paper in a sunny place. Arrange the objects in a decorative pattern on the paper. Can your grandchild imagine what will happen? Wait for a few hours and check on his hypothesis.

Dairy Magic
3 years+

Supplies: ½ pint of whipping cream
Clear container with a tight-fitting lid

Help your grandchild pour the whipping cream into the jar and fasten the lid tightly. Take turns shaking the container of cream until it turns into butter. This can take up to 30 minutes of gentle shaking. At first, it will seem like you are only making whipping cream. Then you will hear gentle "thuds" as denser material hits the sides of the container and the solids and liquids separate. During the final five minutes of shaking, the butter actually turns yellow.

Pour off any excess liquid. Spread the fresh butter on good bread or toast. Enjoy.

It's Raining, It's Pouring
3 years+

Supplies: One-quart glass jar
Plastic ruler
Scotch tape
A day that looks like rain

Tape the ruler to the inside upper rim of the jar so that the 1-inch marking is toward the bottom of the jar. Set the jar outside in the open to collect the rain. While waiting for the rain to fall, go to the library to search for books on rain like Peter Spier's wordless picture book entitled *Rain* or Judi Barrett's *Cloudy With a Chance of Meatballs.* After the rain, run outside to see how much rain has fallen. Stomp in a puddle.

What's That Sound?
3-10 years

Supplies: Small, identical containers with lids
             Objects that make sound when shaken

Grandma prepares this experiment before the grandchild arrives. Save containers such as pill vials, film canisters, or baby food jars or purchase small plastic containers. (Clear containers should be covered with masking tape or paper.) Grandma fills pairs of containers with objects that make a sound when shaken. Examples include: beans, macaroni, sugar, buttons, small nails, paper clips, dirt.

Have your grandchild shake each container and pair them up by sound. Then your grandchild can mix up the containers and Grandma can try sound matching.

Marshmallow Buildings
4-10 years

Supplies: Large marshmallows
             Miniature marshmallows
             Round toothpicks

Show your grandchild how to link marshmallows together with toothpicks to make a building. You can begin with a square and then add more floors and more rooms. Make marshmallow people to live or work in the buildings, using a toothpick to dot food coloring for eyes, mouth and nose. Save the leftovers for S'Mores.

Suggested books are *Building a House* by Byron Barton (2–4 years); *Amazing Buildings* by Kate Hayden (4–8 years); *Castle* by David Macaulay (7–10 years).

Invisible Secrets
4 years+

Supplies: Lemon juice
Sunlight or a light source
Paper
Cotton swab or small paintbrush

Squeeze lemons for juice or use bottled lemon juice. Use the cotton swab or paintbrush to write a secret message on the paper. Dip your brush in lemon juice for each letter. Allow the paper to dry for about 30 minutes.

To read the message, hold the paper up to the sun or to a light source. The invisible message will reappear.

Egg Heads
4 years+

Supplies: Eggs
                     Small quantity of grass seed
                     Potting soil
                     Permanent markers
                     Buttons for eyes, optional

Crack eggs in two pieces, keeping one part of the shell larger. Pour the eggy contents into a bowl and refrigerate for scrambled eggs. Fill the large piece of eggshell with potting soil. Sprinkle grass seed on top of the soil. Sprinkle a thin layer of potting soil on top of the grass seed. With markers, your grandchild can draw a face on the filled eggshell and glue on buttons for eyes, if desired.

Set the eggshells in egg cartons for support. Keep in a well-lit place, watering the grass seed often. The grass seed will sprout and grow in about 5-10 days transforming the eggshell into a critter with hair.

To make a base for displaying the egg heads, glue a 1½-inch strip of heavy paper into a circle. These critters make unique spring table decorations.

Pompeii
4-10 years

Supplies: Clean, empty baby food jar
Play dough
Red food coloring
Baking soda
Vinegar
Tray or cookie sheet with sides

Place the jar, open end up, in the center of the tray. With the play dough, your grandchild can build a mountain around the jar. Add a few drops of red food coloring and one tablespoon baking soda to the jar. Then pour in vinegar and watch what happens. When the volcano dies down, add more vinegar.

Sense of Scents
4-10 years

Supplies: Small, identical containers
Variety of items with a noticeable smell
Scarf or dishtowel

Before your grandchild's arrival, fill pairs of containers with aromatic items such as cinnamon, coffee, vanilla, basil, flower petals, dish soap. Blindfold your grandchild. Can he match up the two containers that smell alike? Can he identify the smell?

Salty or Sweet?
4-10 years

Supplies: Small bowls
             Variety of foods
             Scarf or dishtowel

Prepare the bowls ahead of time with one food per bowl. Include a variety of flavors and textures such as pickles, potato chips, sauerkraut, fudge, or tapioca pudding.

Blindfold your grandchild and offer the foods one at a time for tasting. Talk about sweet, salty, and sour as well as smooth, slimy, lumpy and rough. Can she identify each food, the different flavors, and the different textures?

Un-Electrical Exploration
5-10 years

Supplies: Old electrical equipment

Save any broken or no-longer-used electrical equipment instead of tossing it in the garbage. Items that are fun to explore include a toaster, a computer, a fan, or a radio. Cut off the cord. Let your grandchild imagine how it works by taking it apart. An excellent resource is *The New Way Things Work* by David Macaulay.

True or False
5-10 years

Supplies: Television

Watch a children's television show with your grandchild, paying special attention to the advertisements. Ask him questions about the advertised products. "Do you want to buy the item?" "How did the advertiser make you want to buy it?" Depending on the age of the child, you could discuss truth and exaggeration, business and profit, or other relevant advertising questions. The fun of this activity is watching him discover that not all toys or cereals are as wonderful as advertised.

Christopher Columbus I
5 years+

Supplies: Paper
                    Markers, pencils, crayons

Encourage your grandchild to make a map of her room, a map of her walk to school, or a map of her yard. In a map of her yard, for example, she might draw in the trees, a bicycle, the curves in the sidewalk.

This map-making activity can become more complex. For example, she can create a map from Grandma's house to her house.

Convince Me
5-10 years

Supplies: Simple household item
                       Tape recorder or video camera, optional

Present your grandchild with a familiar object such as an apple, a paperclip, or a ceramic owl. Ask her how she would sell the item on television. What would she say to convince others of the usefulness or beauty of the item? Tape record or video tape her ads. This activity is great fun with more than one child.

An older grandchild could make a craft or a baked item and then develop an ad to convince others to buy it.

Christopher Columbus II
7 years+

Supplies: Itinerary for a car trip
                       Road maps
                       Highlighter

Any long car trip can be accompanied by a place-to-place itinerary so your grandchild can follow along. Encourage him to plot the route on the maps with a highlighter and give directions to the driver.

Grandma's Notes and Ideas

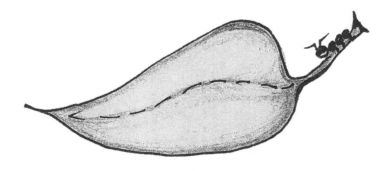

Grandma's Secret Stash
6 months–10 years

Supplies: Special drawer, cupboard, or container
Age-appropriate games and toys

Stock the space or container with wonderful games and toys that your grandchild doesn't have at home. If you have saved *your* child's toys, books, or games, this is an opportunity to re-use them. Add new items as your grandchild grows. Watch her race to the Secret Stash every time she arrives.

Safety and Security Deposits
2–10 years

Supplies: Grandchild's personal items

Have your grandchild leave a number of personal items at your house such as pajamas, a toothbrush, a few favorite books, games, or stuffed animals to be used and enjoyed during his visits. His familiar items make the trip to Grandma's house filled with both expectation and routine.

Camp Grandma
3 years+

Supplies: Grandchildren
                 Longer stay at Grandma's house
                 Pre-planned activities
                 Snacks and meals

Your grandchild will delight in stay-over camp called Camp Grandma, a time at Grandma's house without his parents. Camp Grandma can be an elaborate week-long experience or a simple overnight. You can make it a special event for one grandchild or you can invite several grandchildren for the same period of time. The older children can serve as "junior counselors."

In preparation for your grandchild's visit to Camp Grandma, you can devise an application form that asks him about his food preferences, his favorite activities, his fears, his ideas for fun, or any other pertinent details. You can include a list of possible camp activities and ask him to select his favorites. You can send along photos of Camp Grandma and of its counselors – you, Grandpa, and your pet. In addition, you can ask the parents to fill out the necessary emergency information. Send the forms to your grandchild via snail mail or e-mail. With assistance from his parents, he can return his application to you prior to his Camp Grandma stay.

By using the ideas in *Celebrate!* and by searching for ideas on the Internet and at your local library, you can pre-plan activities and gather the necessary supplies. You may wish to structure each day in a "camplike" fashion setting aside time slots for various activities: Arts and Crafts, Nature, Rest Time, Games, Cooking, Rest Time, Story Time, or whatever activities you prefer. Or you may decide to allow your grandchild to choose the timing of activities. Remember to include rest time. It is a very important activity for Grandma!

Although Camp Grandma involves lots of work, it may become a highly anticipated, annual tradition.

My Grandma's Knickknacks
3 years+

Supplies: A shelf, a box, or Grandma's special drawer

Allow your grandchild to search through a shelf or drawer of Grandma's special items such as dollhouse miniatures, cast iron cars, handmade wooden toys, or pop-up books. With close supervision, you may introduce your grandchild to your collections of glass animals, stamps, coins, bells, or antique dolls.

Good Night, Sleep Tight
3 years+

Supplies: Yarn or fabric
Knitting needles, crochet hook or sewing machine
Polyester stuffing
Embroidery floss

Does your grandchild visit your home for overnights? Imagine his excitement when his special friend greets him each time. Use your creativity to make a stuffed bear or other animal, one for each grandchild, that will remain at your house. Patterns can be found online or in your favorite craft store. If you have several grandchildren, consider embroidering each child's initials somewhere on the stuffed animal.

Grandma's Notes and Ideas

Hi, Grandma
Newborn–3 years

Supplies: Grandma's cash stash

Buy a speaker phone for your grandchild's family so that you can talk to your grandchild even before he can hold a phone. If you have a special game you play with him, you can say it over the phone. "Here comes Grandma's tickle bug. Tickle, tickle." Recite his favorite nursery rhyme or sing his favorite song. If he has a favorite noisy toy at your house, he'll love to hear it over the phone.

You've Got Mail! I
Newborn–10 years

Supplies: Computer with e-mail access
                           Printer and paper

If Mom or Dad sends Grandma regular news about the grandchild via e-mail, Grandma can print up each of these reports. For example, the parent e-mails, "Susie has been teething for ages, but today a beautiful little tooth appeared." As a year or two of these printed e-mails accumulate, take them to the local print shop and have them bound into a spiral book. Read them to the grandchild when she comes to visit or give the book to the parent as a record of the child's growth and development.

Book Gifting—A Tradition
Newborn–10 years

Supplies: Purchased children's books

When visiting a long-distance grandchild, make a tradition of taking along a book appropriate to his age and interests. Write inside the front cover about why you chose this book at this time. For example, if your grandchild is fascinated by the moon, select a book about the moon. Write in the book about the beautiful full moon the two of you saw on your night hike. The books with inscriptions become a chronicle of your relationship as well as a library for your grandchild.

Growing Up with Baby
Newborn+

Supplies: Grandma's cash stash for two webcams*
             Broadband or DSL connection to the Internet

Buy a webcam for yourself and for the baby's family. You can see and talk to the baby "live." Various Web sites offer free access to this service. In this way you can participate in the baby's milestones without leaving your armchair. You may want to set up the system and try it out before the birth so as not to miss one precious moment.

*Newer computers have built-in webcams.

Getting to Know You I
6 months+

Supplies: Video camera or digital camera
             Computer with Internet access, optional
             Compact disc, optional

Make a video of Grandma, Grandpa and pets. (On many digital cameras you can make a brief video.) Send the video to your grandchild via e-mail or on a compact disc. If you have the appropriate computer software, you can add voices and sounds like the dog barking or your voice.

A more elaborate version would be a digital slide show of you and your spouse going through your day: feeding pets, getting in the car, vacuuming, eating dinner, any activities you wish to share. You can narrate it or add music.

Getting to Know You II
6 months+

Supplies: Photos
Picture frame
Photo album with plastic sleeves, optional

Photographs are a great way to keep Grandma, Grandpa, and other relatives on the "front line" at the grandchild's home. Try any of the following:

- Frame a collage of photos (or just one) of Grandma, Grandpa, and pets. Send it to your grandchild.
- Purchase a "talking" frame (available online) to send Grandma and Grandpa's voices along with the photo.
- Make a book of family photos using an inexpensive photo album with plastic sleeves. When you are visiting, play the game "Where's Grandpa?" "Where's cousin Lulu?" Encourage the child to search the pages to find the appropriate person. When she begins to talk, encourage her to name each relative.

Family Foto Fun
6 months+

Supplies: Grandma's cash stash
Computer with Internet access

Make photo books by uploading your photos to an online service. Snapfish, Kodak, and Shutterfly provide a variety of photo services. Following the directions on the Web site, you can create a unique photo book for your grandchild. Possibilities are an alphabet book (A for Cousin Anna), a birthday book documenting the child's parties, or a book about a visit to Grandma's.

A Story Treat
18 months–5 years

Supplies: Computer with a writable compact disc drive
Computer software for recording
Compact disc
Children's book to read
Microphone

Record a story for your grandchild using computer software and a compact disc. If you are not computer-savvy, use a tape recorder, making certain that your grandchild has her own tape recorder. Read a children's book aloud. Use a bell (or voice sound) to tell your grandchild when you are turning the page. Send the book and the compact disc (or tape) to your grandchild.

You've Got Mail! II
3 years+

Supplies: Computer with e-mail access

During your grandchild's visit, assist him with reporting to his parents via e-mail about what's happening during his visit.

With his new awareness, Grandma and Grandchild can keep in touch by e-mail between visits.

Reading Together
3-7 years

Supplies: 2 webcams
                     2 computers
                     Books

Using webcam communication with your grandchild, read a book to her in "real time." Hold the book up to the webcam to show your grandchild the pictures on each page.

For an older grandchild, purchase two copies of the same book. Send one copy to your grandchild. On the webcam, you can read it together, Grandma reading one page, your grandchild reading the next.

A webcam is also a wonderful way to listen to your grandchild's first musical piece or watch her practice for a dance recital.

Where Do You Live?
4-10 years

Supplies: Puzzle of the United States
                     Permanent marker

Purchase a puzzle of the United States in which each state is a piece. Put the puzzle together yourself, marking on it where you live and where your grandchild lives. Place the pieces back in the box and send it to your long-distance grandchild.

You can mark on the puzzle the location of other relatives. You can put the puzzle together with your grandchild and ask what he wants you to mark on the puzzle.

Granny-a-Day
5-10 years

Supplies: An attractive container
                   Heavy-weight paper
                   Grandma's creativity

Begin by collecting sayings or quotations suitable for the age of your grandchild. Type up the sayings and print them out on good-quality paper. Cut them apart.

Purchase a decorative container with a lid or an opening. You might choose a wooden box, a box that you have collaged with photos, or a cookie jar. Fill it with the quotations you have chosen. Have your grandchild select one quotation or saying each day.

Ideas for quotations:

- Find wonderful lines from children's books.
- Search your memory for maxims your own mother or grandmother used. "Waste not, want not" is an example.
- Search the Internet for appropriate quotations.
- Write out "instructions" to your grandchild such as "Laugh at least once today."
- Note how much you love your grandchild such as "You are the shining light in a dreary day."

Grandma's Notes and Ideas

Pretty Toes
Before birth

Supplies: Grandma's cash stash

Treat Mom-to-be to a pedicure and/or a manicure. She will want her nails to look great on the delivery table! You might want to make an appointment for yourself at the same time. Grandmas need pampering too.

Baby Book Club
Before birth

Supplies: Purchased books
              Bookplates, optional

Send a book to the baby-to-be for each month of gestation. Grandma's gift books are a good start for the new grandchild's library. If you wish, use purchased bookplates or write your own inscription inside the book. Keep a list of books that you have given to each grandchild to avoid duplication.

Super Suppers
Before birth and after

Supplies: Grandma's easy-to-prepare recipes
Freezer bags or freezable containers

Moms and Dads of newborns spend little time thinking about or preparing food. They have more important tasks. If the grandchild is close by, you can prepare the food in your own home, freeze, and deliver to the parents to defrost as needed. If you are traveling to visit the newborn, bring copies of your favorite recipes to prepare and freeze while Mom and Dad are occupied with the baby.

Welcome to the World
Before birth or after

Supplies: Pen
Good handwriting

Offer to address the envelopes for the birth announcements.

Peace and Quiet
Newborn+

Supplies: Baby and a buggy

Offer to take the new baby for a long walk so Mom and Dad can have a few moments to themselves.

Baby Soothers
Newborn+

Supplies: Grandma's cash stash

Buy baby her very own MP3 player with speakers. You can load it with some of your favorite music in soft rock or soft classical. Or you can purchase lullabies. The MP3 player can reside in the baby's room to provide a calming and soothing environment before bedtime. Some babies are comforted by "white noise" that can be purchased and loaded on to the player as well.

Cozy Cocoon
Newborn-1 month

Supplies: Swaddling blanket

Babies love to be swaddled. If you will be visiting a new grandchild, bring a swaddling blanket, which is larger than a receiving blanket. Swaddle the baby as in the illustration below.

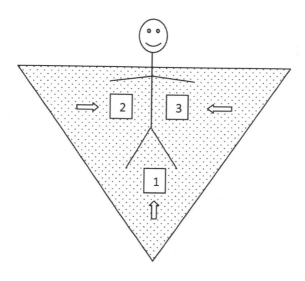

Pretty Patterns
Newborn–4 months

Supplies: Grandma's attention to pattern about the house

Experiment with objects and patterns that capture your grandchild's attention: a fire in the fireplace, pets, books, or colorful toys. Wear patterned clothes or chunky jewelry. Do tummy time on patterned quilts or fabrics. Blow bubbles above and in front of the baby so he can watch the movement.

New Grandma Snuggle
Newborn–6 months

Supplies: Grandma's arms

Grandma loves to snuggle her grandchild on her shoulder. Some babies might prefer a different position. Try holding the baby facing the world instead. Walk around the house talking about objects and patterns you both see.

Sing-A-Long
Newborn–2 years

Supplies: Compact disc
Children's songs or lullabies
Computer software for making
CD labels, optional

Purchase lullabies, soothing songs, or activity songs from an online music Web site and download to your computer. Transfer the music to a disc. You can purchase software kits that allow you to personalize the compact disc with the baby's photo and to make a cover insert.

Grandma's Notes and Ideas